The Den in the Woods

Written by Sarah Loader
Illustrated by Maru Vargas

Spike often went playing in the woods. He was too small to go on his own, so Laura would walk him there. Paul and Jim came too, because they said Laura was also small.

The tall trees made the woods all dark – but Spike was not afraid!

There were lots of sticks that had fallen from the trees.

"Let's make a den!" Laura said to Spike.

Spike looked at Laura as she made walls for their den, and got ferns to make a roof.

It was a lot of work. Paul and Jim got the bigger sticks. Spike could not help because he was too small.

Laura got into the den with Spike.
She called to Jim and Paul.

"Come in!"

Spike laughed at Jim and Paul crawling in.

Spike went flying through the air!

Spike slept.
He was always sleepy after flying.

Soon, it was time to go.
Laura began to pack up.

Laura, Jim and Paul started to walk home.

"Shall we make a big den at home?" Paul asked.

"Yes!" Laura said.

Laura thought of all the things they could do!

Oh no! Spike was still in the den! "Laura!" he called, but it did not work. Spike did have fun in the den, but he did not like being all alone.

Then there were footsteps ...

... but it was not Laura.

The people spotted the den. Then they spotted Spike!

"Hi Spike! I am Kwan," he said.
"I will play with you!"